Focus Guru

104 Awesome Networking Tips

Rachael Chiverton & Jenny Leggott

"I have known Rachael through networking for many years - we have both been members of a national networking organisation, and on the voluntary teams that help to run it. In that time, Rachael has built successful meetings & teams, and is brilliant at connecting people and actually using her network. Seeing beyond the meetings as the only purpose of networking for your business is essential to get the best return on your investment. Rachael is fantastic at making sure that those she networks with get the most of their networking experience, the most out of their investment in networking, and how it can help them get focussed on their networking. These tips will be invaluable to help you get the most from your networking as they come from someone who has done exactly that herself. Rachael walks the walk."

Sheena Whyatt, KAPOW! Your Super Business Coach

"Jenny is a wonderful networker, she gets stuck into meetings as a team member, supports other groups and encourages people with things like roadtrips, turning meetings into destinations for others."

Kirsty Grimes, Love Your Biz Club

"I met Jenny through networking and I'm so glad I did. She's just one of life's most amazing people. Everyone knows that if Jenny says she's going to do something she will do it and if she can't she probably knows someone who can!"

Paul Newton, Mental Theft

"If you ever want to find someone who does XX, ask Rachael! Not only does she have a vast network, she's also always ready to help people within her network, or those new to her network, find meaningful connections."

Sian Rowsell, Sian Rowsell Coaching and Training

"Jenny's experiences and knowledge are legendary. Her ability to help others shows she fully understands the concept of how to get the best out of your time networking."

John Holden, Cabiz Networking Group & Academy

"I met Jenny through a networking event in 2020, and what struck me immediately, was how included Jenny makes everyone feel. We went on to then travel to a networking event several hours away and having those hours in the car meant I could truly absorb just how welcoming and interesting Jenny is as a person. With extensive skills in bringing people together, having asked me a few questions about myself, Jenny was immediately able to reel off names of people she felt I should connect with for business. We have become firm friends, yet Jenny still amazes me with her natural ability to bring the right people together at the right time, definitely a born networker."

Natalia Valentina, Wild & Free To Be Me

"Jenny works hard to make people feel at ease as soon as you meet her. A natural networker, always looking for ways to help others and always on the lookout to pass on opportunities too. A great lady that I feel privileged to know."

Mike Turner, Greater Life

"I virtually me Rachael at an online meeting, back in 2020, during COVID. I was offered the chance to be the Group Leader of a weekly online meeting, 4N Online, Down Under, which Rachael hosted. Rachael was amazing as she put in 150% effort to ensure I succeeded. Rachael also introduced me to many other people who are now great friends. Rachael is passionate about Networking, who I highly recommend because you will not be disappointed."

Mel Jensen, Mel's Customised Candles

"I met Jenny some years ago at a 4N meeting. She was enthusiastic and helped me connect with new people to build my business."

Lesley Watts, Professional Networker

"I've known Rachael for some time and she is a brilliant networker. Rachael is always polite, informative and very welcoming."

Mel Baum, WCR Debt Collection

Focus Guru 104 Awesome Networking Tips

The moral right of Rachael Chiverton and Jenny Leggott to be identified as the authors of this work has been asserted in accordance with the Copyright, Designs and Patents Act 1988.

Copyright © 2022 Rachael Chiverton & Jenny Leggott

First published in 2022

ISBN: 9798846793590

This book is sold subject to the condition that it shall not, by way of trade or otherwise, be lent, resold, hired out or otherwise circulated in any form of binding or cover other than that in which it is published.

It is not intended to provide personalised advice and the authors disclaim any liability, loss or risk incurred as a direct or indirect consequence of the use of any contents of this work.

No part of this publication may be reproduced, stored in a retrieval system or transmitted in any form or by any means without the authors' prior written permission.

All rights reserved.

ABOUT THE AUTHORS

Rachael Chiverton

When not running online and in-person networking events and connecting people, Rachael helps organise people's minds through mindset and time management. She offers administration assistance to clients who try to do it all.

www.getfocus.guru

Jenny Leggott

Alongside writing blogs, business tips and content for clients, Jenny (writing as JT Scott) has published over 30 books for children, including Sammy Rambles, Molly Manila and Bumper and Friends stories and children's activity books.

www.transcendzero.co.uk

Cover Design by Jonathan Smythe, Smooth Designs

As an award-winning art director, Jonathan helps individuals and businesses bring creative ideas to life.

www.smoothdesigns.co.uk

Contents

OUR INTRODUCTIONS 12

THE JOURNEY 14

WHY 104 TIPS? 15

SECTION 1: PRE-MEETING 18

1. REMEMBER YOUR PARKING COINS 20

2. SMALL CHANGE FOR CHARITY POTS 21

3. FOCUS ON WHERE YOU ARE GOING 22

4. CHECK THE POSTCODE 23

5. CAR PARKING 24

6. PLAN TO ARRIVE EARLY 25

7. GET YOUR BUMF TOGETHER 26

8. ROLLER BANNERS 27

9. YOUR BANNER'S WIND-UP KEY 28

10. WHAT CLOTHING ARE YOU WEARING? 28

11. REMEMBER TO PACK YOUR PROPS 29

12. PRACTICE YOUR INTRODUCTION 30

13. PRACTICE IN FRONT OF A MIRROR 31

- 14. PLAN YOUR DAY 31
- 15. QUESTIONS? PICK UP THE PHONE TO THE ORGANISER ... 32
- 16. DO YOU HAVE A TAG LINE? 33
- 17. PRACTICE PUTTING YOUR BANNER UP 34
- 18. CAN YOU TAKE ONE BANNER OR MULTIPLE BANNERS? .. 35
- 19. FOLLOWING UP 36
- 20. FIND THE RIGHT ROOM 37
- 21. SMILE 39
- 22. INTRODUCE YOURSELF TO THE MEETING ORGANISERS ... 40
- 23. CHECK YOU KNOW THE MEETING FORMAT 41
- 24. CHAT WITH PEOPLE 42
- 25. ADD VALUE 43
- 26. OFFER TO GET COFFEE 44
- 27. HANDSHAKES AND HUGS 45
- 28. OFFER TO HELP THE TEAM SET UP 46
- 29. BE KIND 47
- 30. PUT YOUR BUMF OUT 48
- 31. ASK FOR 1-TO-1S 49
- 32. NEVER TURN DOWN A 1-TO-1 50

33. HAVE CONFIDENCE	52
34. GET YOUR BEARINGS	53
35. WATCH YOUR MAKE-UP	54
36. CHECK YOUR BREATH	54
37. TURN YOUR PHONE OFF	55
38. WHERE TO PUT YOUR BANNER (FACE TO FACE)	56
39. WHERE TO PUT YOUR BANNER (ONLINE MEETINGS)	59
40. ALLOW TIME TO PUT YOUR BANNER UP	59
41. BANNER ETIQUETTE	60
42. ARRIVE EARLY TO PUT YOUR BANNER UP	62
43. SHOW SOMEONE HOW TO PUT A BANNER UP	63
44. PUT A BANNER UP FOR SOMEONE	65
SECTION 2: IN THE MEETING	66
45. BE ENGAGING	68
46. DON'T SAY I'M FINE OR I'M OK	69
47. BE PRESENT IN PERSON AND IN THOUGHTS	70
48. SHOW PEOPLE THE WAY	71
49. IT'S OK TO BE NERVOUS	72
50. DONE IS BETTER THAN PERFECT	73

51. COLLECT CARDS FROM OTHERS 74

52. GIVE CARDS TO OTHERS 75

53. LISTEN MORE THAN YOU SPEAK 76

54. ARRANGE FURTHER MEETINGS 78

55. SHARE A WIN OR GOOD NEWS STORY 79

56. CELEBRATE OTHER PEOPLE'S GOOD NEWS 80

57. ALWAYS BE SUPPORTIVE 82

58. NEVER SELL 83

59. BE YOURSELF 84

60. BE ON BRAND 85

61. ASK FOR REFERRALS 86

62. SAY THANK YOU 87

63. ALWAYS HAVE YOUR BUSINESS CARDS WITH YOU 88

64. BE ORGANISED 90

65. BE MEMORABLE 91

66. ALWAYS TURN UP 92

67. TAKE NOTE OF BUYING SIGNALS 93

68. GIVE MORE THAN YOU GET 94

69. FIND OUT MORE ABOUT THEM AS A PERSON 95

70. BE READY TO GIVE UP YOUR SEAT 96

71. WATCH OUT FOR FOOD SPILLAGES 97

72. HAVE FUN 98

73. WHERE POSSIBLE PLAN YOUR BATHROOM BREAKS 98

74. JUST BEFORE YOU SPEAK 99

75. SAY YOUR NAME AND COMPANY NAME TWICE 100

76. GIVE RECOMMENDATIONS 101

77. ALWAYS LOOK BEYOND THE ROOM 102

78. GO WITH THE MINDSET TO HELP OTHERS...................... 103

SECTION 3: POST MEETING AND FOLLOWING UP 104

79. DON'T LET LIFE TAKE OVER 106

80. ARE YOU A BUSINESS CARD COLLECTOR? 107

81. FOLLOW UP EVERY 1-TO-1 108

82. THANK THE PRESENTER AND THE ORGANISERS 110

83. POST A REVIEW ON SOCIAL MEDIA 112

84. ADD PEOPLE TO YOUR MAILING LIST AND USE IT! 114

85. ALLOW TIME FOR EMAIL AND PHONE FOLLOW-UPS 115

86. IT'S NOT JUST BEING IN THE ROOM 115

87. ORGANISE A SOCIAL OUTSIDE OF THE MEETING 116

88. THE FORTUNE IS IN THE FOLLOW-UP 117

89. PICK UP THE PHONE 118

90. DO WHAT YOU SAY YOU'LL DO 119

91. ADD PEOPLE TO YOUR CRM 119

92. WOULD YOU LIKE TO SPEAK AT THIS EVENT? 120

93. BUILD RELATIONSHIPS 121

94. HELP PUT OTHER BUSINESSES IN TOUCH 122

95. LOOK FOR COLLABORATIONS IN THE SAME INDUSTRY .. 123

96. CONTACT YOUR IDEAL CUSTOMER TO ATTEND 124

97. TALK TO ANYONE AND EVERYONE 125

98. RUN A MEETING 126

99. GIVE A PRESENTATION 128

100. GET ON A TEAM 132

101. DO YOUR POSTS, BEFORE, DURING, AND AFTER 136

102. WOULD YOU SCRAP YOUR PRINTED BUSINESS CARD? 137

103. WINDOWS, LIGHTING AND BACKGROUNDS 138

104. NO "LAP" TOPS 140

BONUS TIP! 141

ACKNOWLEDGEMENTS 142

Our Introductions

Lots of people go to lots of networking events for lots of different reasons. Some people are keen to make sales, others are keen to make friends, and a great many of us do both.

Rachael's networking journey started in March 2014.

"I was attending a training course on Twitter and got chatting with the trainer. They suggested I try networking for my new business Rachael Chiverton Ltd. so I booked into a networking meeting the following day and loved it!"

Within 6 months Rachael was not only getting clients from networking, but she was actively involved in running 3 fortnightly meetings and gained many local friends as well.

Since then, Rachael counts networking as an integral part of her business and hopes readers of this book will gain valuable insights to enhance their networking skills.

Jenny's networking journey started a few years earlier in 2006 when she was looking for ways to promote her employer's business and a friend suggested attending the first 4Networking meeting in the country.

"I was so scared! Everything from what to wear, what to say, where to park, what to expect, I had a million questions and looking back I'm surprised I actually turned up but glad I did as it led to some amazing business contracts, great ideas when setting up my own company, and best of all, some lifetime friends."

Over the years, Jenny has joined several networking teams and carried out roles from behind the scenes to front of house.

She also counts networking as a vital part of business life and hopes some if not all of these tips help others make the most of their networking experience too.

We hope you enjoy reading
   "Focus Guru - 104 Awesome Networking Tips".

Rachael & Jenny

The Journey

Living at nearly opposite ends of the country you might think it wasn't possible to meet, let alone become great friends and write books together, but that's exactly what's happened!

Rachael and Jenny met at the 4Networking meeting run in a posh hotel in Cheadle in 2018. It was an evening meeting and sitting at the same table gave Rachael and Jenny the opportunity to chat.

"We had lots in common," says Jenny. "We connected on Facebook and have been able to meet in person every so often."

In 2020 Covid struck, and face-to-face networking moved to online-only meetings. Through her role with 4Networking, Rachael suggested setting up a new "Dog Lovers Networking" meeting, bringing people with a passion for dogs all over the UK together via Zoom and it was at one of these meetings where Rachael and Jenny decided to write the Focus Guru books together.

Why 104 Tips?

We agree, 104 tips is an unusual number! But, it's one of the trademark signs of the Focus Guru books to have a symbolic number in the title.

When carrying out the research for this book and drawing on Rachael and Jenny's collective experiences, recalling many stories and incidents from meetings, there was easily enough material for several books!

"We wanted to create a comprehensive networking guide to satisfy any questions from those who have never been to a networking meeting right the way through to seasoned networking professionals who we hope will recognise many of the topics we cover and see them again through the eyes of a first-time visitor."

Having attended and run many meetings Rachael is often asked about how to make the most of networking, especially from people who are struggling, or who don't feel like networking is working for them.

Rachael says: *"With our shared love of meeting people through the networking circuits, it made perfect sense to write down our real-world experiences, both of attending meetings and the work carried out behind the scenes."*

Jenny says: *"We hope you'll find this book is a great resource for making the most of your networking experiences. We've worked hard to include a wide range of pre-meeting, at-the-meeting, and post-meeting tips that are easy to read and easy to use."*

Why 104 Tips?

Put simply, it's memorable and divides nicely into 2 tips per week for readers who enjoy reading books in bitesize chunks!

Focus Guru – 104 Awesome Networking Tips

Section 1: Pre-Meeting

Section 2: In the Meeting

Section 3: Post Meeting & Following Up

Section 1: PRE-MEETING

These are the tips for your pre-meeting planning.

Yes, this is the bit where you get really organised ahead of whizzing out of the door to get to your next meeting!

Our first tip is something that's often overlooked but can be frustrating if you haven't got any.

You might wonder why we start with something so simple, but remember, this book is aiming to cover everything you could ever want to know about networking and the tips are for everyone to enjoy whether you're a newbie or a seasoned pro.

PRE-MEETING PLANNING

Coins

1. Remember Your Parking Coins

> ➢ Coins for parking meters are one of those things that gets overlooked and can be a source of stress and frustration when arriving at a networking venue.

> ➢ You might find the parking meter has a "Pay By Phone" or "Pay By Card" feature, but having a small stash of coins available can be very helpful.

> ➢ On this note of parking, another tip is to know your vehicle registration mark (especially if hiring a car or van) as some parking meters ask for this as well as your money.

2. Small Change For Charity Pots

➢ On the same theme of having a few coins with you is that the opportunity may arise to drop coins or notes into a charity pot passed around by the organiser or one of the attendees. Usually this is advertised in advance and you can choose whether to participate or not.

Getting There

3. Focus On Where You Are Going

- ➢ It might sound obvious but focus on knowing where you are going, or you might end up somewhere else!

- ➢ How long will it take to get there (allowing time for traffic) and do you know your route?

- ➢ Make sure you have a contact number for the meeting organiser in case you get stuck in traffic or need help finding the venue.

4. Check The Postcode

- It's really important to make sure the postcode actually takes you to the venue.

- Using an Internet-based map, such as Google Maps, can help find the exact place where you need to be.

- There's nothing worse than checking online and confirming the postcode is correct only to get into your car to start the journey and find the postcode doesn't exist on your in-car Sat Nav.

Rachael says: "I run a networking meeting in Manchester and if you use the postcode it takes you to the wrong side of the dual carriageway! To overcome this, my team and I remind attendees to use the venue name instead."

---

5. Car Parking

- ➢ It pays to check if the venue has its own car park and how long the car park can be used for.

- ➢ Or alternatively, where is the nearest car park (and is it coin, card, or phone payments)?

- ➢ Remember to save the venue and car park location in your satnav before you set off so it's easy to find at the beginning and end of the meeting.

6. Plan To Arrive Early

➤ There is possibly nothing worse than rushing into the meeting and everyone turning to look at you because you've been stuck in traffic, you got lost on the way, or didn't check the postcode.

➤ By arriving early you'll have extra time for networking and making new friends and business connections.

➤ You're also likely to be able to meet the team running the meeting and have extra 1-to-1 time with more people.

Jenny says: "By arriving early and leaving late you might get an extra hour of free networking time for your business."

Things To Take With You

7. Get Your Bumf Together

- ➢ Bumf is a networking term used for things you might want to give away, things to show people during your business introduction, or hand out during the meeting.

- ➢ Examples of bumf can include leaflets, business cards, product samples, books, pens, coasters, and other promotional items.

8. Roller Banners

➢ A roller banner is a brilliant way to get your message out to a wider audience. It's your silent salesperson advertising your products and services, even when you're not in the room.

➢ You may also find your roller banner appears in other people's photos taken at the meeting and that's a bit of free advertising for you.

➢ Depending on your budget and how much you can carry, you might consider having multiple roller banners in a banner wall or positioned strategically at the meeting.

9. Your Banner's Wind-up Key

- On the subject of roller banners, did you know they come with a wind-up key, a lifesaver if your banner doesn't roll up easily.

- Typically you'll find your wind-up key in the small space used for the folding pole.

- The wind-up key is used on the side of the base to turn the banner material around the spindle, and then it will fit back into the carry-case!

10. What Clothing Are You Wearing?

- To be visible, recognisable and memorable, wearing your work uniform, company colours, branded shirt, shorts or cap are great ways to reinforce your brand at networking meetings.

11. Remember To Pack Your Props

➢ Closing the tips on "Things To Take With You" we recommend packing any props you wish to use for your business introduction so that they're ready to use in the meeting.

Rachael says: "I take a soft toy squirrel with me to meetings and use it in my business introduction. I've done it so many times that people shout 'SQUIRREL' at the right time!"

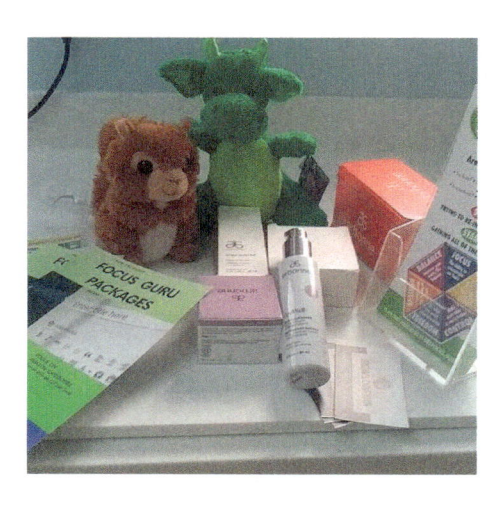

Preparation

12. Practice Your Introduction

- ➢ In the meeting, do you know if you will have just 20 seconds, 40 seconds or 60 seconds to make your business introduction?

- ➢ Make it count! Be informative. Be funny. Be factual. Be You. Leave people wanting to know more about you and your business.

- ➢ Try to keep your introduction simple, keep it to one product, or perhaps to one company (if you have multiple businesses).

- ➢ Remember, you can use your 1-to-1 meetings to tell people more about what you do.

- ➢ It's tempting, but don't reel off everything you do in your business introduction, especially a long phone number!

13. Practice In Front Of A Mirror

➢ While you're practicing your introduction, try doing it in front of a mirror or a trusted friend. Do you look happy, nervous, grumpy? How do you think you will come across to others?

14. Plan Your Day

➢ Allowing plenty of time for the meeting, and for staying for an extra few minutes afterwards, means you won't be upset if you can't get a 1-to-1 with "that person". Maybe they can stay for an extra few minutes at the end too and you'll still get time to chat or to arrange a follow-up meeting.

➢ Allowing the extra time in your schedule will help make the rest of your day go smoother as you'll have taken the pressure off needing to be at your next destination.

15. Questions? Pick Up The Phone To The Organiser

➢ Are you unsure of anything about the upcoming meeting?

➢ Is there something you want clarification on?

➢ Pick up the phone and call the meeting organiser.

➢ Remember, the organisers will want you to be at the meeting so it's in their interest to make sure you feel confident when you arrive, rather than a room full of nervous networkers who won't get the most out of the meeting and who probably won't come back!

➢ Most networking meetings will have phone, email and social media contact details with real people answering.

➢ If you have a question, it's much better to ask!

16. Do You Have A Tag Line?

➤ Lots of businesses have tag lines, the words you are almost programmed to associate with their products and services.

➤ A tag line can be a great way to finish your business introduction, something relevant and memorable works well.

Rachael says: "My tag line is 'Giving you your time, your way, with no SQUIRRELS' and people in the room often shout 'SQUIRRELS', so it works!

I also get tagged on social media in photos of squirrels, and there was a time when someone said they thought of me when their Dad's dog chased a squirrel in the park!"

---

17. Practice Putting Your Banner Up

➢ How many people actually practice putting their banner up in the office or at home? Maybe not many, but it can be helpful to be skilled at putting up and taking down a roller banner.

➢ Proficient roller banner assembly (and putting away) means you'll be quicker at it in the meeting and you'll be able to focus on chatting with people at the networking meeting.

➢ Another reason to practice is to make sure your banner is in good condition, with no rips or tears which can look poor and can influence how people perceive you and your business.

➢ Also, if there are any special techniques to getting your banner back into the carry-case, you'll know them inside-out.

18. Can You Take One Banner Or Multiple Banners?

➤ Some networking meetings encourage multiple banners, and some might prefer one banner per person, it's always worth checking.

➤ For each banner you take, remember to allow extra time to set them up. You might find it takes about a minute per banner, or a bit longer if you're chatting with someone at the meeting while putting your banner up.

➤ If you're not sure how long you'll take, try timing yourself as you might not be as quick in the meeting as you are at home or in the office.

19. Following Up

- Yes, it's strange to write about following up in the preparation stage of this book, however you'll find following up is probably about 80% of any networking meeting.

- Back to making sure you have time for things, make sure you allow time for an email follow-up and/or phone follow-up ideally the same day or within 24 hours of the meeting.

- You'll be surprised how many people attend meetings and then vanish, only to be seen at the next meeting!

Following up is probably about 80% of any networking meeting!

On Arriving

20. Find The Right Room

- It's all very well arriving at the right time at the right venue, but it's also important to make sure you're in the right room!

- If it's not obvious which room you need to be in, or what floor it's on, ask for help. There will usually be someone on the reception desk and don't worry about asking for help, we are all first-time visitors at some point!

- Plus, once you know the layout of the venue you'll be able to help someone else in the future and, who knows, maybe that conversation will result in a new friend, business connection, sale or purchase.

- When you're in the right room, just check it's the right meeting!

Here's a story from Rachael about getting the right room and how to make the most of the unexpected!

"I was running a meeting in Stockport and one attendee asked at reception where she would find the networking meeting. She was directed to a room and spent 45 minutes eating breakfast and chatting. The penny dropped when someone asked, 'so what are your views on construction?'

CONSTRUCTION! The lady was a dog walker looking to advertise her business. She was in the right venue but at the wrong meeting!

It turned out alright in the end as she found Rachael's meeting and was only a few minutes late.

Plus this savvy dog walker made the most of the unexpected opportunity to meet more people and got business connections from both meetings!

The lesson here is to always check when you arrive in the room that you're in the right room."

21. Smile

➢ When you enter the room make sure you walk in with a smile (and sometimes it's good to wave as this movement gesture helps people notice you, even if you're not waving at anyone in particular).

➢ Smile when you introduce yourself to the meeting organisers (you might know them, but they might not know you, yet).

➢ Smiling is completely free, but its value is priceless.

➢ It puts you in a positive frame of mind, no matter how slow the traffic was, or if you were in the wrong room, or if things are in chaos elsewhere in your life, if you can smile, even if it's a small smile, it will make a big impact.

22. Introduce Yourself To The Meeting Organisers

➤ This is a great way to get known within a new networking group as the organisers are in touch with everyone who attends.

➤ Remember, the organisers might be people who run businesses too and they might also keep you in mind for introductions, referrals and socials.

➤ Don't just introduce yourself once, do it every time and you'll soon make new friends and business connections.

23. Check You Know The Meeting Format

➢ Not all networking meetings are the same so it's always worth checking the order of events.

➢ The core features, such as the opportunity to introduce yourself and your company, a presentation and 1-to-1s or mini-meetings, are included in many networking meetings, but they may be performed in a different order, or the meeting may have some new features since the last time you went.

➢ If you know the meeting format you'll be able to spot the best time to make an urgent phone call, to time a comfort break, to swap a business card, or top up your coffee.

24. Chat With People

> Remember, everyone who goes to a networking meeting is a real person. Everyone has a life outside of the meeting. Ask them about things happening in their life!

> Easy starting points are to ask where they live, do they have pets, what do they do?

> You may find you have shared hobbies. Perhaps you have a mutual love of boats or cars, support the same football team or went to the same place on holiday last year. Maybe you have children of similar ages, or have the same breed of dog, cat, or horse.

> You'll almost always uncover a topic of interesting conversation.

> If you really can't think of anything else, you can always chat about the weather!

25. Add Value

➤ Adding value is something that's often talked about, yet if you ask people about it you may sometimes get a glazed look, as though they don't know what value they might be adding, and that's ok!

➤ Value means something different to every one of us.

➤ Think of it as what extra you can offer, something that might be helpful.

➤ Adding value could be something tangible like saving money off an electric bill, or something simple like showing someone where the coffee machine is.

Always be on the lookout for places where you can add value to conversations with others.

---

26. Offer To Get Coffee

- Speaking of coffee, offer to get coffee for someone (if it's free, or if you can afford to pay for one if it's not).

- Offering to get coffee is a nice icebreaker, especially if you're nervous or don't like standing still while chatting.

- Equally, saying "I'm going to get a coffee" is a simple and polite way to extract yourself from a conversation if you want to be somewhere else.

- Don't fall into the trap of going to get coffee on your own if you wanted to chat with the person you offered the drink as they might be in another conversation when you return!

- Suggesting coffee is a good way to chat privately with someone away from the main networking group if you have something confidential or sensitive to discuss.

27. Handshakes And Hugs

➤ It's one of the unwritten networking rules about how to greet your fellow networkers.

➤ You'll soon work out who shakes hands, who likes to give hugs (informally known as "huggers"), and those who do neither.

➤ Watch closely for non-verbal cues and give someone their space if they don't want your early morning bear-hug!

28. Offer To Help The Team Set Up

- This tip can earn brownie points as there's always lots to do at the start of a networking meeting.

- Easy things to help with are putting up event roller banners, moving tables and chairs if needed, and it never hurts to offer to get coffee!

- It also makes you visible and memorable to the team who are likely to be well connected on the networking circuit.

- Should the opportunity arise to recommend you or refer someone to you, you'll be favourably on their mind.

- Plus, it gives you a soft-start getting valuable experience for the future if you want to form your own team and run a meeting too.

29. Be Kind

➢ This follows on from helping and being a nice person in general. It's easy to find fault with others - maybe they're late, scruffy, disorganised, clumsy or rude. Maybe they had problems getting to the meeting or have something going on at home.

➢ You have the choice to be kind and you're sure to get back what you give out.

30. Put Your Bumf Out

➢ We covered "Bumf" in one of the earlier tips and hopefully you'll have arrived at your networking meeting with a few things to hand out and put on the designated bumf table.

➢ Unless you're encouraged to do so, don't put your bumf on every chair or every place setting. It can be overwhelming, a nuisance if there's no room to put down a plate of food, and most likely it will end up unread and in the bin.

➢ Ask the organisers if there's a bumf table or somewhere you can put your bumf. They may say it's ok to put your bumf on every place setting but typically it's poor etiquette and not very environmentally friendly.

➢ Popular bumf items are brochures, flyers, business cards, pens, coasters, keyrings and chocolates with your company branding.

31. Ask For 1-To-1s

➢ Never be afraid to ask someone for a 1-to-1 at a meeting. They might be the Managing Director or on their first day at a new job, everyone has attended with the purpose of networking and seeking out new connections and new business.

Never be afraid to ask for a 1-to-1 meeting.

32. Never Turn Down A 1-To-1

➢ There might be an exception to this tip, but in general never turn down a 1-to-1 with someone if they ask you for a 1-to-1.

➢ You might not want a repeat 1-to-1 if you had a 1-to-1 with them last week. Maybe you think they'll never be a client, or they don't know anyone who wants what you do.

➢ But, it can be a real kick for someone who might have had to summon a lot of courage to ask you for the 1-to-1. Maybe they're someone who has just been refused a 1-to-1 by someone else. Maybe they forgot they had a 1-to-1 with you last week.

➢ If you don't want a 1-to-1 with someone during the meeting there are some "get outs" where people might say "sorry I'm out of 1-to-1s", or "sorry, I've pre-arranged my 1-to-1s", or you can offer a 1-to-1 outside of the meeting.

➢ And, you never know, maybe they wanted to chat with you about a multi-million pound contract, you never know, so try and always take that 1-to-1 and see where it leads.

Never turn down a 1-to-1 meeting with someone as you never know where the conversation might lead.

33. Have Confidence

- Did a parent ever tell you to "stand up straight", "put your shoulders back", "take a deep breath", "sip water before you speak", "project your voice to the back of the room"? In networking meetings this advice makes all the difference how you are perceived in the room.

- Sometimes you can make yourself look more confident by faking confidence. It's easier said than done, but very effective. Have confidence! You know what you do!

- If you're worried about speaking in public just remember the 20 seconds, 40 seconds or 60 seconds for your introduction is over very quickly and you can enjoy listening to everyone else.

- Some people have a preference whether they go first, last, or not at all, if you're concerned about speaking in front of the whole room, mention it to the organisers so they can put you at ease.

Jenny says: "At my first meeting I remember writing my introduction out on paper word for word. When it was my turn I managed to read it out but my hands were shaking so much with nerves I couldn't hold a knife and fork for a minute or two afterwards as they were clanging really loudly on the plate as I tried to eat!"

34. Get Your Bearings

- ➢ When you arrive it can be really useful to find out the location of the toilets, coffee station and nearest exit.

- ➢ These are questions someone might ask you and it's helpful to be able to share the information when asked.

- ➢ Knowing where things are can help you to feel more relaxed when you arrive at a meeting.

35. Watch Your Make-up

> At networking, as with life in general, watch for lipstick on your teeth, other people's cheeks, collars, and clothes.

> It might take many minutes to put on your fabulous make-up, but it can take just a second for it to rub off on someone's shirt if you go in for a hug!

36. Check Your Breath

> Check your breath before, during and after the meeting, to give out the right signals.

> If you wish, you can get small boxes of mints with your company logo (great for bumf tables) to share with your networking group.

> The golden rule is never turn someone down if they offer you a mint – it could be friendly, flirty, or a subtle hint that your breath smells!

37. Turn Your Phone Off

➢ Either switch your phone off, put it on silent, or turn on Aeroplane Mode.

➢ You're either there for networking or if you need to make and take calls, it's nice if you can do it outside of the main networking area.

Rachael says: "People on their mobile phones at networking meetings is one of my pet-hates. I find it really rude and hate it if people make or take non-urgent calls. You've got voicemail for taking messages. Networking meetings are still business meetings after all."

Banners

38. Where To Put Your Banner (Face To Face)

➢ Think carefully about where you place your banner in the networking venue - why are you taking a banner in the first place? It's to be seen!

➢ If you want to help people understand who YOU are and what YOU DO, try and put your banner behind your chair so people associate you with your banner and consequently with your products and services.

➢ If you want to get the maximum number of attendees looking at your banner then a popular hover-spot is to put your banner by the drinks station. Everyone getting a drink will have the opportunity to see your banner.

➤ If you want to get the maximum exposure of your banner on other people's social media posts, place your banner behind the speaker as most people take a photo of the speaker during the presentation, and your banner will be in all the social media posts.

➤ If you want your banner to be seen by everyone coming and going through the venue, place it by the main entrance or check-in desk. You may find you're competing for floorspace with the networking event banners, but it's still a good spot for visibility and awareness.

➤ Try to know the reason for bringing your banner and find the best spot for it during your networking meetings.

➤ No matter where you put your banner, make sure you do use it and it doesn't just sit in your car or van!

Jenny says: "A top tip for banners is to put your carry-bag next to or underneath your banner. This helps at the end of the meeting when everyone packs up their banners to know whose carry-bag is whose!"

Rachael says: "My top tip is to put your business card in the window of the carry-bag and Sellotape it so it doesn't fall out. This helps you to know which banner is which if you have more than one banner and it also helps other people know whose carry-bag is whose too!"

39. Where To Put Your Banner (Online Meetings)

➤ If you're at an online networking meeting you can still make good use of your roller banner by placing it behind you.

➤ This works twofold, it hides any clutter in your home or office and reinforces your company brand when your camera is on.

40. Allow Time To Put Your Banner Up

➤ We mentioned earlier about allowing time to put up your banner and the same goes for online meetings. Get it done before you click to join the meeting so you can arrive online with your "silent salesperson" already set up in the background.

➤ Remember to allow more time for multiple banners. It takes a minute or two to get the banner out of the bag and set it up, but it's definitely worth doing even for short meetings.

41. Banner Etiquette

- ➤ If you have multiple banners you can create a "banner wall" but make sure there's room for everyone to put their banner up.

- ➤ Beware of the "Banner Bites Back" scenario! Occasionally accidents can happen when setting up or taking down a roller banner.

- ➤ Always check the space around you when setting up, taking down, or moving a banner to avoid causing injury to anyone, especially with the metal poles!

- ➤ Be ready to move your banner if asked by the organisers as they will want to make sure the banners aren't blocking any exits, that the banners aren't a potential hazard, and also to make sure everyone has a fair opportunity to put their banner up at the meeting.

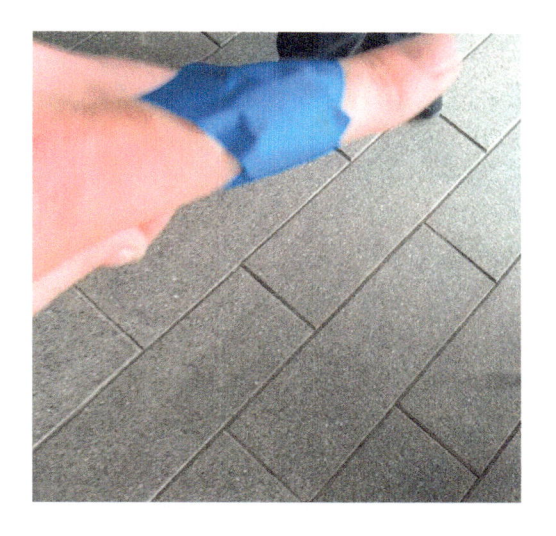

Rachael says: "After 8.5 years with no incidents there was a meeting where my banner fought back as I was putting it up. It took a chunk out of my finger and I needed a plaster from the venue.

Imagine how much I would have remembered them if a fellow networker had produced a plaster at that moment Why don't you be that person and carry a first aid kit ready to help others?"

42. Arrive Early To Put Your Banner Up

➤ It helps to arrive a few minutes early to set up your roller banner.

➤ You'll get first choice of the best spot in the venue to set up your banner.

➤ Plus you'll have plenty of time to chat without the distraction of putting up a banner at the same time.

Roller banners are a great way to advertise your company, your products and your services.

Arriving early makes sure you have first choice where to put your banner up!

---

43. Show Someone How To Put A Banner Up

➢ There are a great many different ways to put up and take down a roller banner and no-one knows all of them!

➢ Some banners have a helpful arrow sticker in the middle to show you where to place the pole.

➢ Most banners have a hole in the base to place the pole for extra stability. There's also the compartment for the wind-up key, but hopefully you won't need to use it.

➢ Could YOU show someone an easier way to put up their banner?

Rachael and Jenny both take roller banners to meetings but through writing this book discovered the way they put the banners up is completely different!

Rachael says: "I don't fold the feet out first, I connect the pole and put it in the base, then I lean the banner backwards until I can easily reach the top. Then I pull out the banner, connect it to the top of the pole, stand the banner upright, then I pull the feet out.

Jenny says: "I fold the feet out first, take out the pole, put my foot on the base, unroll the first couple of feet of the banner, then unfold the pole using it to raise the banner to its full height, secure the pole in the hole in the base and wrap my carry-bag around the pole to finish.

44. Put A Banner Up For Someone

➤ At some networking meetings the team will have four or five banners to put up as well as banners for their own company, so if you see the team are busy setting up the room, have they left their banners on the floor ready for putting up?

➤ Can you help put up banners for the team?

➤ Are you a tall person? Could you help someone shorter than you to put up their banner?

➤ Take a look around the room – is there anyone who looks anxious or procrastinating putting their banner up? Maybe they're nervous or maybe they don't know how to do it.

➤ Could you help by offering to put up their banner for them or showing them how to do it?

Section 2: IN THE MEETING

These are the tips for when you're in the meeting itself.

Yes, this is the bit where you get to find out the best tips to make the most of being at your meeting!

Our first tip in this section is something that can be overlooked but is the foundation of being memorable at meetings and a sure way to make new friends and business connections.

You might wonder why we start with something so simple, but remember, this book is aiming to cover everything you could ever want to know about networking and the tips are for everyone from newbie to seasoned pro.

IN THE MEETING

45. Be Engaging

> What does it mean to be engaging? Everyone is different but being engaging means to be there in mind as well as in body at the meeting.

> Pay full attention to those you're with while you're with them. Everyone has a story and if you allow yourself to fully listen to their stories there's a good chance they will listen to yours.

> What do you say to be engaging? Well, this can start with simple things like making good eye contact, a smile or asking an open question.

> How you stand can signal engagement, is your body language open and welcoming, or are you consciously or unconsciously holding back?

> Do you light up the room? You'll know from the way other people treat you, if they come up to you for hugs or handshakes, to ask questions or give compliments.

46. Don't Say I'm Fine Or I'm OK

➢ If someone takes the time to ask how you are why wouldn't you give them an honest answer?

➢ If you say "I'm fine" or "I'm OK" it can close off a conversation. Remember, people buy from people and none of us are perfect!

➢ If you're having a tough time, many people will have been in your position or they know someone going through something similar, and it's OK to share things if you feel comfortable doing so.

➢ Networking meetings are for people to meet and chat. They're designed to be a supportive environment. Someone might have an answer to your worry, stress or problem.

➢ Equally, it's OK to say "I'm OK" or "I'm fine" if you are but do try to follow it up with more details so the conversation carries on.

47. Be Present In Person And In Thoughts

- This carries on from the tip on switching off your mobile phone during a meeting.

- Clear your mind from any distractions.

- Forget about the pile of washing at home, or the way the traffic might be dreadful on the way back to the office.

- Forget any of your recent arguments or upcoming appointments.

- Simply focus on the here and now.

- You'll find it easier to concentrate on the people and conversations at the networking meeting if you can be present in person and in your thoughts.

48. Show People The Way

➢ Yes this is your chance to be extra helpful! You can direct people to where food is being served or to the toilets.

➢ You might be surprised how important food is at meetings, so if you have extra details about what type of food, where it is, when it is available, what you can choose and any special dietary choices, people will thank you!

➢ You can be friendly and welcoming and people will remember you.

Rachael says: "In my experience running networking meetings, the top 5 things people want to know are where to find coffee, where to sit, where to put their banner, where are the toilets and when is the food coming!"

---

49. It's OK To Be Nervous

➢ Remember, everyone was new once.

➢ Everyone gets nervous sometimes.

➢ A few nerves can be a good thing.

Rachael says: "I remember the introduction I did at my very first networking meeting. It was short, simple, but very effective:

*'I'm Rachael.
I help people get paid.
I'm Rachael.'*

and then I sat down!"

---

50. Done Is Better Than Perfect

➢ Would you agree it's better to get something done, even if it's not perfect?

➢ This goes for introductions and presentations, emails, phone calls and social media posts.

➢ If you wait for "perfect" it might never happen.

You'll find an example of "Done Is Better Than Perfect" on page 94 of Focus Guru 52 Ways To Achieve Your Work Life Balance where Rachael had just a few hours to prepare a science talk that was brought forward by a few weeks when the keynote speaker dropped out at the last minute.

Another example is when Rachael was given 2 days notice to give the main presentation at a meeting in Stockport. She wrote and delivered "From Dream To Published In Under 5 Months", an engaging 20 minute presentation based on Focus Guru 52 Ways To Achieve Your Work Life Balance and sold 4 of the books to people in the room.

51. Collect Cards From Others

- It's good to collect business cards from people at networking meetings for many reasons.

- You'll have their contact details to arrange further chats and meetings.

- You're at a networking meeting to meet people so it makes sense to gather their details.

- You'll find people want to give you their details as they are at a networking event too!

- It's good etiquette to accept a card from someone even if you don't think you'll speak with them or trade with them.

- Maybe they have a reason to give you their card, and it could be a subtle way that they want you to reciprocate and give them your card.

52. Give Cards To Others

➢ Just as you take the cards that are given to you, feel free to give other people your cards too.

➢ If you're not sure how to do this, or if you're a bit nervous, just drop it into the conversation, "may I give you my card" or "shall we do a card swap" are easy questions to ask.

➢ Your business cards are likely to have your name, title, company, website, email, social media links and phone number. These are all useful pieces of information for people to contact you in the future.

➢ If someone does refuse your card, or if they leave it behind or, perish the thought, you spot them putting it in the bin, don't worry! There will be many people who will make good use of having your contact details.

53. Listen More Than You Speak

> Silent is an anagram of listen.

> You have two ears and one mouth, use in these proportions.

> It's hard to listen while you're speaking.

> In 1-to-1 meetings, make sure you share the time. You'll learn more about the other person if you give them the opportunity to talk.

> Beware of someone doing the same to you! If you spot someone is trying to listen more than they speak, try asking open ended questions, or chat about hobbies, family, pets, the weather, anything to get a two-way conversation going.

> During presentations it's bad form to interrupt the speaker, unless heckling is encouraged.

➢ It's also considered bad form if you're chatting with your neighbour during the business introductions. Your neighbour might want to listen to the introductions and why should anyone listen to you if you won't listen to anyone else?

➢ Equally it's considered bad form to chat with your neighbour during the presentation stage. Someone has gone to the trouble of writing and delivering the presentation and it's courteous to listen or pretend to listen even if the topic isn't necessarily relevant to you.

➢ Listening more than speaking can be a good way to add positively to your reputation within the networking group.

People like to talk, but they also like to be listened to.

54. Arrange Further Meetings

- Don't be fooled that everything happens within the boundaries of the networking meeting. If anything, more often happens after a meeting has taken place.

- Arranging further meetings gives you the chance to explain more about what you do. It gives you the chance to learn more about another networker.

- In further meetings you're likely to be able to spot opportunities for collaboration, referrals, recommendations, socials and more.

- It takes time to get to know people and the more layers you can build into your networking relationships you'll find they quickly become long-lasting, more productive and enjoyable ways to do business together.

- What can you offer to make the further meeting better for both of you?

55. Share A Win Or Good News Story

- If you can bring a good news story to your networking meeting it has many benefits both to you and to your networking group.

- It can make you feel good to recount a win or recent success story and gets good endorphins going in your mind.

- It encourages others to bring their good news stories to the meeting and lifts the mood in the room.

- Sharing a win is great! Don't be afraid to share your success and be happy for others when they report good news in your group too.

- Examples can be sharing the news that you've won a new contract, you're celebrating a work anniversary, or a new baby in the family.

56. Celebrate Other People's Good News

- Even if you're not feeling great, try to celebrate other people's successes. They will remember those who stood up and cheered and those who frowned and turned away.

- If you can't be happy when someone else does well, why should they be happy when it's your turn to celebrate a win?

- Some networkers have families and friends who can't or don't understand their business and who don't appreciate the good news and wins.

- Networking might be the only place where you and your business are understood, so it makes sense to celebrate everyone's good news.

Rachael says: "One of my great networking friends arrived at a meeting and he was over the moon because he had just finished installing the flooring in his new office. His family couldn't understand why it was important, but it was a great good news story and we all stood up and cheered!"

57. Always Be Supportive

➢ If someone has shared a problem or difficulty with you it may have taken a lot of courage to share what's happening in their life.

➢ Whether you can help or not is a something you can decide depending on the situation.

➢ Always be friendly and welcoming, especially if there's someone new joining your group.

➢ Networking meetings thrive on attendance so it makes sense to make sure everyone has the support they need. Put yourself in their shoes.

➢ Congratulate people on their successes.

Jenny says: "We usually save seats for first-time visitors next to team members so there's always someone on hand to answer any questions."

58. Never Sell

- This is a grey area because most people go to networking meetings to sell their knowledge, products and/or services.

- Remember, people like to buy but they don't like to feel like they've been sold to.

- The golden rule is to avoid being, or being seen to be, pushy.

- Do ask for the sale. There's nothing wrong with asking for the business. If someone says "no", stop there. If someone says "maybe later" or "I'll think about it", stop there.

Jenny says: "I've had success offering my children's books for people to buy at networking meetings and I've met people who are experts at closing big deals there and then. It comes down to offering people the right thing at the right time rather than outright selling."

59. Be Yourself

- If you're not yourself, who are you?

- Be yourself because you can't be anyone else.

- Be genuine and true to yourself.

- Realistically, there's no-one everyone likes so don't try the impossible!

60. Be On Brand

➤ In networking meetings it's absolutely fine to wear your company branded t-shirt, jumper, coat or hat, to drive your company branded car and write notes on your branded notebook with your company logo on your pen.

➤ The words you speak, the clothes you wear, the props you use, keep them all on brand for maximum visibility and memorability.

Rachael says: "I always wear my black and white wrap with a badge with my logo on the collar to meetings. It's comfy and people know it's me."

Jenny says: "When I'm promoting my children's books, I take the books and brightly coloured soft toy dragons with me. At meetings I've been called 'The Dragon Lady' and that's OK because it's memorable!"

---

61. Ask For Referrals

- Always ask for referrals. The worst that can happen is you get a "NO!"

- It's not pushy to ask for a referral, you're not asking for a sale or an order, you're asking someone if they know someone who might like your products and/or services.

- You're not asking people on the street or cold calling anyone. It's simply asking people at a meeting who in their network they can add value to by referring you to them.

- You don't have to call it a referral, you can simply ask "do you know anyone else who might like <insert the name of your product or service here>" and listen to what they say.

- Make it a habit to ask people for referrals as you never know where your name will come up! Giving other people referrals is good too.

62. Say Thank You

➤ There are lots of opportunities to thank people at networking and in life in general.

➤ You can thank someone for asking how you are, or how your holiday was, or how your family are, you can thank them for getting you a tea or coffee, or for giving you directions.

➤ Thank you goes a long way.

"Saying thank you doesn't cost anything, but it means masses to the other person." - Focus Guru – 52 Ways To Achieve Your Work/Life Balance

Jenny says: "When I was younger, I remember being told 'please and thank you are magic words that make things happen' and it's true!"

63. Always Have Your Business Cards With You

➢ Remember to take your business cards with you and you might be surprised how often you use them and exchange them with others.

➢ So people know your phone number.

➢ So people can get your email address.

➢ So people can remember your name.

➢ So people can remember your company name.

➢ Your business cards can show your title and position within your company.

➢ Business cards with relevant contact details can help direct enquiries to the correct person.

➢ If you have matt-finish cards people can make notes on your cards, e.g. a further meeting date.

➤ Virtual business cards can be useful and environmentally friendly, however not everyone has a QR reader on their phone and not everyone wants everyone they meet in their phone book.

➤ If you have a photo of yourself on your card it can be extra memorable for people.

Rachael says: "I was at a conference in Edinburgh and on the second day a delegate came up to me and said 'I got loads of business cards last night and yours is the only one I know who gave it to me as it's got your photo on it!' so it works!"

---

64. Be Organised

➢ Being organised can give you extra confidence when arriving and entering a meeting.

➢ Being organised will help you in the long run, it will save time, create a better impression and help you get the most out of your networking.

➢ Don't turn up with a scruffy carrier bag, unless you need it as a prop.

Jenny says: "When thinking of examples of being organised, one tip is to carry your bag or banner in your left hand to leave your right hand free for handshakes."

Rachael says: "I always plan to arrive early so I can find out where the speaker will be and then put up my banner in that area so it will appear in more photos."

65. Be Memorable

➤ What can you do to make yourself memorable? Make sure you're memorable for the right reasons, not the wrong ones!

➤ Rachael often gets tagged in photos and video clips of squirrels as she's known as "the lady who banishes squirrels* from the working day".

➤ If you're using a prop, make sure it's relevant to what you do otherwise it can be confusing.

➤ Being memorable comes in all shapes and sizes. It can be what you wear, what you say, how you treat people.

➤ Being memorable is as much about you as it is about your business.

Squirrels are cute animals that can easily distract us and make us stop what we're doing, so banishing squirrels is like banishing distractions from your goals and objectives.

66. Always Turn Up

- ➢ Unless there's a reason not to turn up, it's always worth getting to your networking meeting even if you're running late.

- ➢ Don't be the only name-tag left on the welcome table when everyone else has arrived.

- ➢ Not turning up can undermine confidence in you and your business that you might not turn up to a client meeting or that you might not carry out work for someone.

- ➢ You're not just a number. Both organisers and attendees at well-run meetings will genuinely care and be concerned if you haven't turned up.

67. Take Note Of Buying Signals

➢ Just because you're at a networking meeting it doesn't mean you can't close deals in the room.

➢ Keep alert for buying signals from the people you're meeting. They might buy from you or refer you to a friend, their family or colleagues.

➢ Buying signals can be "BUY NOW", "Future" or to add notes into your CRM. Stay alert!

68. Give More Than You Get

➤ This tip is fairly self-explanatory, for example, if someone asks you for directions, you can give the directions and also point out a place of interest, where to eat or something they won't want to miss.

➤ You can add value by looking for people you can introduce another attendee to. You can listen to what problems people may mention – can you help them?

➤ When trying to connect people with each other, a caveat is not to give out someone else's contact information unless you have their permission to do so. Simply say, 'if you give me your contact details, I'll pass them on'.

Rachael says: "Don't sell at people. Tell them about the itch you scratch."

69. Find Out More About Them As A Person

➢ What are they doing after the meeting?

➢ Do they have a family? Have they got pets? What are their hobbies?

➢ They are not just a one-dimensional person, there is more to them than just what you see at the networking meeting.

➢ The more you can find out, the more likely lasting friendships will build and you'll find more opportunities will arrive.

➢ People buy from people, not logos or brands, so make sure you're a person, not a machine!

Rachael says: "Always remember you're talking to a person, not a purse."

70. Be Ready To Give Up Your Seat

➢ If you have chosen a seat at the end of a table, or near the toilets or exit that would be more useful to someone else, be ready to give up your seat.

➢ There might be someone who is less able or less mobile than you who might prefer a seat at the end of a table.

➢ If someone is nervous then a seat at the end of the table can be easier than being in the middle where conversations can take place at all angles.

➢ Or if someone needs to leave the meeting early, a seat at the end of the table or a seat near the door can help them leave more easily.

➢ There might be occasions where someone will ask to sit next to their friend or colleague and swapping seats can give you the opportunity to meet someone you wouldn't usually sit with.

71. Watch Out For Food Spillages

➢ Yes! Food spillages do happen and it's how you deal with it that counts.

➢ It's easy to get wrapped up in a conversation or absorbed by the presentation and drop, spill, or knock something. Baked beans are often the culprit!

➢ Beans, runny egg or toast crumbs dropped on a dress, shirt or tie is not a good look!

➢ But don't let that put you off eating at meetings, some people wear patterned clothes or loud shirts for this very purpose (true story).

72. Have Fun

➢ Networking isn't supposed to be boring, stuffy, or a chore, so it's OK to enjoy the meetings.

➢ In some meetings heckling is allowed and even encouraged to create a lively atmosphere.

➢ But be warned, if you take it too far or make it too personal the organiser might have a quiet word or if it's an online meeting, you might get put on mute!

73. Where Possible Plan Your Bathroom Breaks

➢ If you can, make sure you're not the person who needs to run to the bathroom before the start of the presentation or introductions. Plan your bathroom breaks and coffee top-ups.

➢ Of course, if you need to go, you need to go, and the ideal is to leave with discretion without disturbing too many others.

74. Just Before You Speak

➢ In the introductions it can help to take a sip of water before you speak. It helps your voice and gives you a moment to get everyone's attention.

➢ Remember to speak a little louder than usual and project your voice to the back of the room. There might be someone who's hard of hearing and you don't want them to miss what you're saying.

➢ Remember to speak a little slower than usual to give people time to digest what you're saying.

➢ Another tip is to take a few deep breaths before you speak to get more oxygen into your blood and so you don't feel faint when talking.

75. Say Your Name And Company Name Twice

➤ When introducing yourself and your company in the 20 second, 40 second, or 60 second round of introductions, it makes sense to say your name and company at both the beginning and the end of your introduction.

➤ Saying your name and company name at the beginning enables people to know instantly who you are and where you're from.

➤ Repeating your name and company name at the end allows people who weren't listening at the beginning to make a note of who you are, what you do and which company you represent.

➤ It doesn't hurt to repeat your name and company name, in fact the repetition is a great way to secure your presence in people's minds.

➤ Don't worry, you'll probably repeat these details many thousands of times!

76. Give Recommendations

> It's always good if you can give someone a genuine recommendation and a shout-out in the networking meeting.

> When you mention someone by name it gives them a feel-good factor and also puts you in a good light too.

> Another idea is to ask someone you've recently worked with if they'll give you a testimonial or recommendation in their introduction too.

> Reciprocating someone else's recommendation is good, but remember, recommendations can be something you give to some and take from others and you might not get back from the person you gave to.

77. Always Look Beyond The Room

➤ This simply means to look for opportunities where people in the networking meeting might be able to recommend you and your products and services to people they know.

➤ Everyone in the room will have friends, family, colleagues and clients who might want what you do.

Rachael says: "I travelled for 3 hours to give 3 presentations in 3 days. Then 6 weeks later I had a call from someone in Malaysia who had an outstanding invoice they needed help collecting the money from a client in Bradford. When I asked how they'd heard of me I learned it was the person in Malaysia's UK contact who put them in touch with me and he definitely wasn't in the same room! It definitely pays to always look beyond the room."

---

78. Go With The Mindset To Help Others

➤ If you can go to networking meetings with the mission of finding out how you can help others you'll find you reap what you sow.

➤ There's the law of attraction that says you'll attract the friends and clients you think about most, so why not make your thoughts positive and find ways to help others.

➤ Through helping others you'll attract the help you need to further your sales and business objectives.

➤ You might not receive help or advice from those you give your time to, but it's a cycle of giving and receiving, and you'll find you do get as much as or even more than you give.

Section 3: POST MEETING AND FOLLOWING UP

These are the tips for what to do after your meeting has taken place.

Yes, this is the bit where you really get the most out of attending the meeting and follow up with the people you've met to re-enforce your friendships and business connections.

Our first tip is something that often happens but is easily avoided with just a little preparation.

You might wonder why we start with something so simple, but remember, this book is aiming to cover everything you could ever want to know about networking and the tips are for everyone from newbie to seasoned pro.

POST MEETING AND FOLLOWING UP

79. Don't Let Life Take Over

➢ Once the meeting has finished it can be tempting to get straight back to work or to your next meeting.

➢ Make notes during the meeting.

➢ Make notes during your 1-to-1s.

➢ Make notes in your car before driving off.

➢ As soon as you're out of the meeting your phone will ping with notifications, you'll look at text messages and missed calls, and these distractions might make you miss a key piece of information someone said which could be a potential lead.

➢ By making a written or typed note in the car before you look at any other messages or notifications you will remember who you wanted to follow up with and why.

80. Are You A Business Card Collector?

➢ What do you do with all of the business cards you've collected? Do they pile up on your desk?

➢ Are you using digital contact details, taking photos or scanning people's business cards to save paper?

➢ Whichever method you use to collect people's contact details it makes sense to do something with them.

Rachael says: "I recommend you look at your business cards at least once a month and phone people to see how they're doing and then see where the conversation leads."

81. Follow Up Every 1-To-1

- Don't miss anyone when following up with your 1-to-1s. You never know where the next opportunity will come from.

- It doesn't take long to do each follow up and in some meetings you'll have one or two people to follow up with and in other meetings there may be more.

- Make your follow-up email, message or call all about the person rather than an outright sales pitch (unless they specifically said "Yes, Sell To Me Today").

- Following up builds rapport.

- Following up builds trust.

- Through following up it's a natural process to make friends from your networking contacts.

➤ Through networking lifelong friendships can and do form and this leads to another person looking out for leads for you (as you'll be doing for others) as we love to support our friends in business.

➤ The more you go to meetings the more you'll see this in action and a large part of this is founded in following up.

➤ If you prefer not to call it "following up" you can treat it as "checking in" and do this as much for your networking contacts as you would with your friends and family.

82. Thank The Presenter And The Organisers

➢ Give yourself an extra few minutes at the end of the meeting to make a special point of thanking the presenter for their talk during the meeting.

➢ Even if the talk wasn't relevant to you, maybe you found it boring or you'd already heard it word for word at another meeting, the presenter has still given their time and shared their expertise.

➢ Saying thank you is an easy way to make yourself known to the presenter and become a potential source for future recommendations (if you've heard their talk twice or more the chances are the presenter visits lots of meetings and, you never know, they might recommend you to someone further afield).

➢ If you don't have time to stop at the end then send a quick message to say thank you.

➤ Thanking the team and meeting organisers also makes yourself known in the wider networking circuit and being the person who stops to say thank you is better than being known as the person who grumbles about the choice of food!

➤ To make the thank you even more special, try to include one thing you took from the meeting or the presentation (to show you were listening and paying attention!).

➤ Keep in mind the meetings are all run by people and there wouldn't be a meeting to attend if it wasn't for the team running things behind the scenes as well as on the day of the meeting.

Always thank both the presenter and the team, either during the meeting or when you're doing your following-up messages.

83. Post A Review On Social Media

➤ After the meeting, post a review on social media. It's another way to boost your profile within the network and offers a signpost to other networkers who may enjoy coming to the next meeting.

➤ Tag people into the post (tag the people you met and chatted with as well as the organisers and team). You can also tag people who weren't at the meeting as well.

➤ In your review you can write about what you liked about the meeting. Maybe you liked the meeting format or were inspired by the speaker.

➤ Write about anything you gained from the meeting. Did it make you want to learn a new skill, book a holiday, find a new client or simply do something differently?

➢ You can put details of the next meeting date and the next speaker in your review. These are useful details for someone looking at your post to help them decide if they want to attend.

➢ If you took photos at the meeting add them into your post for extra interest. If you and your roller banner are in the photos it's great free advertising!

84. Add People To Your Mailing List And Use It!

➢ In addition to your follow up emails you may wish to set up a mailing list to broadcast your company news on a regular basis.

➢ Add a note into your calendar to remind you to write and send your mailshot at regular intervals.

➢ You don't need to reinvent the wheel when looking for content.

➢ It's possible to write a blog, social media post or article and recycle the content in bitesize chunks for your mailshot.

➢ Using one of the online mailing list systems gives you tools to see how many people have read your mailshot and subscriber options too.

85. Allow Time For Email And Phone Follow-Ups

- You'd be surprised how many people go to networking meetings, then vanish, only to be seen again at the next meeting.

- Allowing time for quality follow-up phone calls and emails is where the magic happens.

- Each conversation you have with someone builds layers of trust and friendship which can turn into solid business relationships.

- Given the choice, wouldn't you prefer to do business with someone you liked speaking with?

86. It's Not Just Being In The Room

- There's a lot more to networking than attending the meetings. What can you do between meetings to further your business friendships and build those layers of knowledge and trust?

87. Organise A Social Outside Of The Meeting

➢ It can be great fun to be the person who organises the socials outside of networking meetings. Don't just leave this to the organiser or the team. Get stuck in and send out some invitations!

➢ What do you like doing? It makes sense to organise a social around something you like and you'll probably find other people enjoy the same thing too.

➢ If you're stuck for ideas, think about what other people like doing. Your social could be anything from a dog walk, a trip to the cinema, a meal out, or going to watch a football match.

➢ Think about what time of the day or night you want to arrange your social and you'll find different people will come along, fitting it in around their home and work commitments.

88. The Fortune Is In The Follow-Up

➤ You might be thinking there's a lot about following-up in this book and there is, because this is where the magic happens!

➤ You'll find the percentage of time between attending networking meetings and carrying out your follow-ups is about an 20/80 ratio.

➤ Following-up enables you to be in the right place at the right time for someone to say YES!

Rachael says: "When does the furniture sale end? Never! That's because they don't know when you'll need a new sofa so the sale has to be never-ending."

89. Pick Up The Phone

➢ Your phone isn't just for checking social media! Use it to make some phone calls or send some text messages.

➢ Make it your mission to telephone 3 networking contacts today.

➢ If you do this once a week you'll soon get through contacting everyone.

Jenny says: "I do a ring-round calling people when I'm travelling to and from the supermarket. It's an hour of travel time so I try to make the most of it and catch up with people I haven't seen or heard from for a while and something always comes out of these ad-hoc conversations."

90. Do What You Say You'll Do

- ➢ Various statistics say only 2% of people actually do what they say they'll do.

- ➢ So, if you do what you say you'll do, you'll stand out and be remembered and networking is all about being remembered (for the right reasons).

- ➢ If you don't take on too much you'll be able to do the things you say you'll do and get a great reputation too!

91. Add People To Your CRM

- ➢ It's great going to networking meetings and collecting business cards, but remember to add them to your Customer Relationship Manager (or CRM for short).

- ➢ Your CRM can be a database or spreadsheet and you can link it to your email or mailing list.

92. Would You Like To Speak At This Event?

➢ There are lots of opportunities to speak at networking meetings and events.

➢ Firstly, know WHY you want to speak at the event. You can use the speaking opportunity to raise awareness of you and your company.

➢ It can be a safe space to practice your public speaking skills.

➢ Use it as an opportunity for receiving feedback on your presentation skills and your content.

➢ It's more free marketing for your company.

➢ Remember to leave people wanting more!

➢ If possible, have a free download or handout at the end, but don't force it on anyone.

93. Build Relationships

> Through regular networking, you'll find many lifelong friendships can and do form.

> These friendships lead to other people looking out for you in life and in business.

> We all love to support our friends and it's a natural process to make friends from your networking contacts if you go to meetings regularly.

> Remember, relationships lead to clients, one-off touches don't.

> People used to need seven touch-points before they buy (e.g. seeing an advert in the paper, receiving a phone call, or opening an email) but now the number is more like seventeen!

Relationships are important.

94. Help Put Other Businesses In Touch

➢ Don't just look for your own clients when you go to networking meetings. You'll find that if you can put two people in touch with each other who need a product or service and who sell a product or service, you'll find both people will remember you.

➢ If you're going to meetings to find your own clients, then only your own clients will remember you.

➢ Also, the more you give, the more you'll get. Many new networkers don't understand the value of this.

➢ Maybe you think it's either counter-intuitive or counter-productive to put other businesses in touch with each other. But it works.

95. Look For Collaborations In The Same Industry

➢ The more you look for collaborations the more you'll find. Is there an event you can do together with another person or their company?

➢ Do you have a slightly different speciality? Can you fill the skills gap for another company?

➢ This book is an example of two networkers collaborating!

Rachael says: "There's a meeting in Stockport where four accountants attend each week. I know for a fact that each accountant has passed work to another accountant as their speciality suited the client better."

---

96. Contact Your Ideal Customer To Attend

- It makes sense to invite people to networking meetings and when sending your invitations, send them to people you would like to meet.

- If you know what your "ideal client" looks like, find lots of them to invite to meetings. You're giving them the opportunity to be in a room with people who might like their services as much as you're giving yourself the opportunity to get to know them better.

- A bonus is that you'll be remembered by your "ideal client" as well as the team organising the meeting. A good team always welcomes visitors recommended to come to their meetings.

- You're adding value to your ideal client and it helps build a stronger relationship with your ideal client. It gives you the chance to have a 1-to-1 chat with them to find out more about how you could do business together or collaborate on a project.

97. Talk To Anyone And Everyone

➢ Remember networking takes place in many different places.

➢ Networking can take place in the actual meeting venue, but it can also just as easily take place in the pub, on a dog walk, when you're out in town, or at a different networking event.

➢ If you see that someone is looking for more business, maybe in a social media post or newspaper advert, pick up the phone and invite them to a networking meeting you're attending.

Talk to people and invite them to come along to your next networking meeting! The more you do this, the easier it gets.

---

98. Run A Meeting

➤ It's not as daunting as it sounds. Running a meeting has far-reaching benefits.

➤ Running a meeting makes you the Go To person for that area.

➤ It gives you a much higher profile within the network and among other networking meetings.

➤ It's a chance to promote your business without outright selling.

➤ It gives you an excuse to contact your ideal clients without selling to them, if you consider it selling, then all you're selling is the idea of coming to a meeting.

➤ You'll receive a much higher profile locally.

➤ It's a chance to showcase your skillset.

- ➤ It's a chance to work within a team. This can be great if you're a sole trader or work alone.

- ➤ You'll receive the tools and training to set up and run successful meetings.

- ➤ You'll receive support and advice from trusted colleagues.

- ➤ It can increase your confidence levels in public speaking as well as other areas of life.

99. Give A Presentation

- There's a presentation or talk inside everyone as everyone has a story to share. Accepting the challenge to deliver a presentation to your networking group can help you become the "Go To" person for your industry.

- It's a chance to showcase your knowledge and your expertise.

- It's a great way to practice your public speaking. You can rehearse at home and deliver it in a safe space as the people at networking meetings have come to listen to what you have to say.

- It can start your journey into becoming a paid speaker.

- You can inspire people at the meeting.

- Your presentation can be business-related or it can be life-related. No one else has been on the exact same journey to get where you are today.

- Always check the length of time you have for your presentation with the team. Some meetings allow 15 minutes, others 20 minutes and some talks can be an hour or more.

- Allow time for questions at the end (or take questions at intervals during your talk) and prepare a couple of questions for the organisers to ask, in case your audience is shy.

- Preparing answers to common questions is a good idea so you'll know the questions are coming and have the confidence to answer with certainty.

- If you're using technology supplied by the venue, always arrive early to check it works.

- If you can, bring a backup of your presentation that doesn't need an overhead projector, or a laptop with slides. Not all venues have these facilities and if they do, they don't always work!

- Think through what you want people to learn from your presentation.

- What are the takeaways you are going to give people? What do you want people to remember afterwards? What is the one thing they will remember about you?

- Have a definite conclusion to your talk so people are in no doubt when it has finished (otherwise how will they know when to clap or give you the standing ovation?).

- Don't make it a sales pitch, unless it's supposed to be, and allowed to be, a sales pitch.

- Leave your audience wanting more.

Jenny says: "I've given different presentations over the years talking about everything from writing my books, to handwriting analysis, to my life journey. It's given me the confidence to become a paid speaker in front of a worldwide audience."

Rachael says: "My presentations are varied and the content is tailored to suit each audience. I've given scientific talks and small business advice covering systems and processes, motivation and accountability, but my favourite talk has to be the quirky titled 'Networking Tips From The Dog' where I combine my love of dogs with real-world networking tips."

100. Get On A Team

- Once you've been to a networking meeting you might find you're approached by the organisers asking if you want to join the team and help with future meetings.

- It's nothing scary and chances are you'll be doing things for the team that you already do in your own business, like making phone calls, sending emails, and making sure everyone's happy!

- Each networking meeting is likely to have some or all of these roles in place:

- **Group Leader** – The front-of-house face of the meeting, the person with the passion and charisma to keep the energy levels up. Ideally this is someone who isn't shy (or someone working on being less shy) and who likes to be in the spotlight. Someone with a big presence but isn't overbearing. Is this you?

- **Group Co-ordinator** – The person who liaises with the venue (for face-to-face meetings) and with the attendees. Typically this is someone who's super organised and customer focussed. One of the usual responsibilities of the Group Co-ordinator is to set up the room, putting out placemats and ensuring the placenames for the expected attendees are on the welcome desk. They might also be responsible for collecting meeting fees, taking a register of attendees, and paying the venue for the food and drinks.

- **Host** – This is the person who selects and trains the team and can offer support to each person behind the scenes. For online meetings, the Host is generally the person with the Zoom account used to run the meeting. They select the venue, agree the timings with the venue, check the costings and requirements from an overall perspective.

> **Visitor Co-ordinator** (or Visitor Cuddler as Rachael likes to call them) – This is your friendly, approachable, all-round nice person. Working with the Group Co-ordinator, they will contact each visitor in advance of the meeting and check each visitor knows the location, the format, what to bring and answer any other questions the visitor might have. A great Visitor Co-ordinator will research each visitor on social media so they'll know what the visitor looks like and can welcome each visitor by name and be ready to introduce them to the most relevant people for them to chat with in the meeting. On the day, the Visitor Co-ordinator will welcome the visitor by name, check they know the meeting format, assist the visitor with finding a seat, or a coffee, or someone to chat with, and make sure the visitor feels comfortable and can get the most out of the meeting.

➤ If you imagine networking as a business, especially in larger networking organisations, there's a structured hierarchy and management.

➤ Each meeting has a team and some of the team members might be on multiple teams running meetings in different locations, or they might be in charge of a geographic area.

There are lots of benefits to being on a team and it doesn't have to be forever.

Our advice is to get stuck in and really enjoy helping make your networking meeting the best meeting on the circuit.

101. Do Your Posts, Before, During, And After

- Speaking of making your networking meeting the best on the circuit, it makes sense to post how great it is/was on social media.

- Do a post before the meeting to let people know your meeting is on and what to expect.

- Do a post during the meeting, preferably with photos, saying what's going on.

- Do a post after the meeting, letting everyone know what happened.

- Each time you post you're boosting your visibility to your audience and potential clients.

- It helps increase the visibility of the meeting, and in turn this encourages more people to attend, and who knows, they might be your future customers.

- ➢ It helps you promote yourself without selling.

- ➢ Tell people you are going, you're at, and you've been to a meeting or an event.

- ➢ Let people know you had a good time (if you did) and how much you enjoyed the meeting.

102. Would You Scrap Your Printed Business Card?

- ➢ Printed business cards have been around for a long, long, time and now there are new methods for storing and sharing business card details.

- ➢ Digital cards can be used to share your details digitally. They can be free, faster and more accurate than typing details manually.

- ➢ This tip is food for thought, it's not something (at the time of writing this book) that Rachael or Jenny have implemented.

103. Windows, Lighting and Backgrounds

➢ In your online meetings there are a few good things to remember about what other people will see when your camera is turned on.

➢ The top tip is to have natural lighting where possible, and for the order to be "window", then your "laptop/desktop/tablet/phone", then "you". If it's bright outside and your window is behind you, you'll end up looking like a talking silhouette.

➢ By using as much natural light as possible you're helping your webcam give a cleaner image compared with the speckly/noisy image as the camera tries to fake light to show you clearer.

➢ If you don't have a window or your meetings are in the evenings, consider buying a ring-lamp, either one that is free-standing or clips to your device.

➢ Keep an eye on your background too, the virtual backgrounds where you fade in and out, or you take a drink from a cup with an invisible hand are amusing but distracting!

➢ By all means go and buy a green-screen and use a photo of the beach if you wish but remember that people buy people so if your background is really a working office, a building site, or your kitchen cupboards, keep it real.

Rachael says: "If you have a roller banner use it as your background for online meetings. It will remind people of who you are and what you do. Plus it's bound to get into some social media photos too!"

---

104. No "Lap" Tops

- ➤ This tip applies mostly to online meetings where you might be tempted to sit on your favourite sofa with your laptop on your knees.

- ➤ Every shift in movement, however slight, makes your camera shake as though you're in the middle of an earthquake.

- ➤ Sitting at a desk is a good way to avoid pet intrusion where your cat might walk across your keyboard or your dog might want to check out your screen.

- ➤ Of course, the number one rule of any pets gate-crashing a meeting is to show your pet to the online room. Let your pet be a celebrity for a moment!

BONUS TIP!

- Don't limit yourself when you start networking.

- Try different meetings at different times of the day, or meetings in different towns.

- Keep trying until you find the best meeting format and group for you and your products and services.

- Remember, it's not just the people in the room, it's all the people they know, and all the people they know, and so on.

- Your networking circle will soon become a large part of your business, whether you're buying, selling, or just along for the ride.

Acknowledgements

We would like to thank a few people for inspiring us to write this book and supporting us on our journey:

4N Online

Without 4N, Jenny and Rachael might never have met! Living 285 miles apart we met face to face when Jenny made the round trip to visit the northern 4N face to face meetings.

https://4nonline.biz

Brad Burton

The friendship was also cemented through Brad's Now What Club. His advice and real-world business lessons have provided invaluable inspiration and guidance.

https://bradburton.biz

Jonathan Smythe

A truly creative genius, whom Rachael and Jenny met through 4Networking. On mentioning writing this book, Jon said, "I love helping friends out, please can I do your cover FOC" and we agreed!

https://www.smooothdesgins.co.uk

Adrian Cuthill and Dominic Fenton

Another chance meeting through 4Networking led to creating Dragonball Sports Ltd. Developing the game from Jenny's books into a real-world sport, yet again proves achieving a work/life balance is possible.

https://www.dragonball.uk.com

If you'd like to find out more about what Rachael does or to book a 1-to-1 or Power Hour with her, visit:

http://getfocus.guru

If you'd like to find out more about what Jenny does with copywriting and children's books, please visit:

https://www.transcendzero.co.uk

Future Books:

Rachael and Jenny are already talking about the next in the series of Focus Guru books. We are really looking forward to working together to create our new book which will be released soon.

https://getfocus.guru/104

Printed in Great Britain
by Amazon